Hello English!

English
Picture Dictionary

D1144166

Contents

2	numbers	16	park	32	party
3	seasons	17	sport	33	clothes
4	at home	18	in the forest	34	zoo
5	in the garden	19	weather	35	under the sea
6	kitchen	20-21	opposites	36-37	beach
7	living room	22	shapes	38	farm
8	bathroom	23	swimming pool	39	farm animals
9	bedroom	24	library	40	describing yourself
10	town	25	stories	41	family
11	vehicles	26	on my desk	42-47	word list
12	supermarket	27	classroom		
13	shopping	28-29	body		
14	fruit	30	actions		
15	vegetables	31	playground		

numbers

1	one	**2**	two		
3	three	**4**	four	**5**	five
6	six	**7**	seven	**8**	eight
9	nine	**10**	ten	**11**	eleven
12	twelve	**13**	thirteen	**14**	fourteen
15	fifteen	**16**	sixteen	**17**	seventeen
18	eighteen	**19**	nineteen	**20**	twenty

| spring | summer | autumn | winter |

365 year   **12** month

January	February	March	April
May	June	July	August
September	October	November	December

roof

garage

chimney

window

door

bin

ladder

ball

path

nest

tree

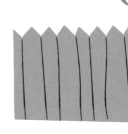

fence

hose pipe

grass

worm

flower

gate

hedge

kitchen

fridge

knife

oven

cupboard

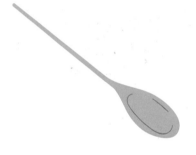

spoon

sink

fork

cup of tea

coffee

telephone

stairs

sofa

cushion

television

games console

ceiling

armchair

floor

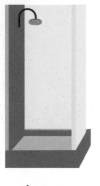

shower

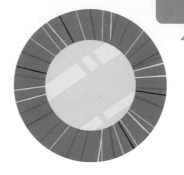

mirror

sink

toothpaste

soap

toilet

toothbrush

towel

bath

chest of drawers

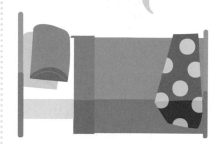

wardrobe

bed

poster

doll

teddy bear

curtains

rug

alarm clock

church

synagogue

cinema

mosque

train station

post office

town hall

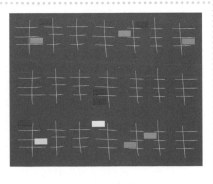

car park

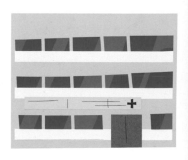

hospital

vehicles

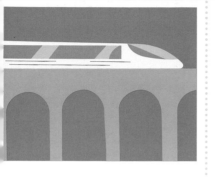

train

motorbike

aeroplane

fire engine

police car

ambulance

car

taxi

bus

supermarket

fishmonger

butcher

money

shopping trolley

shopping basket

shopping bag

till

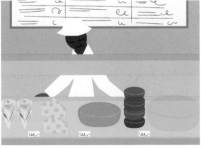

cheesemonger

bakery

milk

rice

eggs

meat

cheese

butter

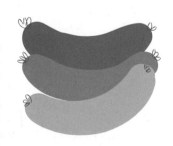

sausages

pasta

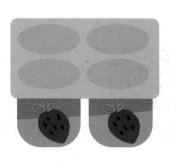

yoghurt

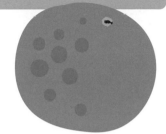

fruit

apple

apricot

orange

grapes

strawberry

raspberry

banana

pear

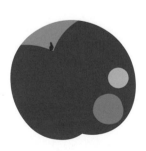

peach

tomato

broccoli

carrot

green beans

courgette

celery

sweetcorn

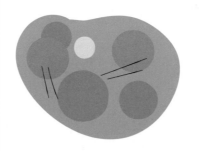

potato

lettuce

lake

bridge

duck

bench

swan

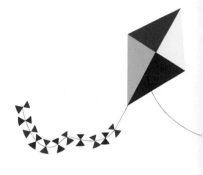

kite

river

dog

ice cream

sport

skateboard

football

tennis

running

basketball

baseball

bicycle

rugby

gymnastics

in the forest

mouse

hedgehog

owl

caterpillar

fox

squirrel

bird

deer

beetle

hot

cold

cloud

sun

wind

fog

storm

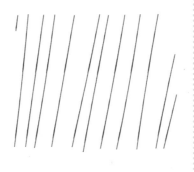

rain

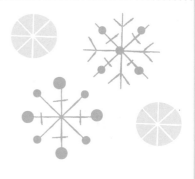

snow

big

small

on top

high up

inside

under

low down

outside

fast

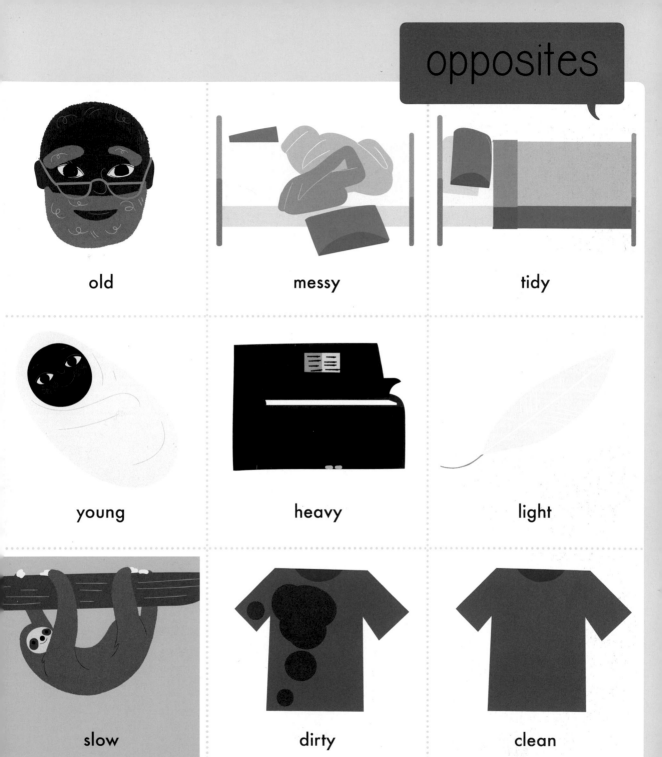

old

messy

tidy

young

heavy

light

slow

dirty

clean

rectangle

rhombus

star

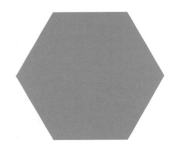

hexagon

pentagon

oval

circle

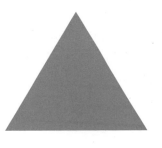

triangle

square

swimming costume

swimming cap

swimming goggles

diving board

shampoo

I am swimming

lifeguard

swimming

armbands

once upon a time

librarian

picture book

comic

storytime

costume

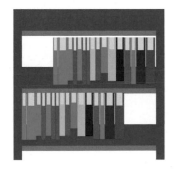

shelf

beanbag

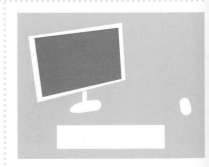

computer

stories

pirate

castle

mermaid

fairy

witch

unicorn

princess

knight

dragon

notebook

ruler

pen

paper

paints

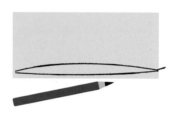

pencil case

colouring pencil

scissors

glue

teaching assistant

teacher

clock

alphabet

book

chair

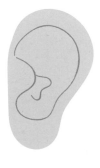

listen

look

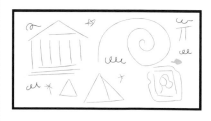

whiteboard

nose

arm

head

mouth

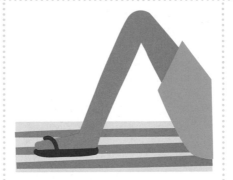

leg

hand

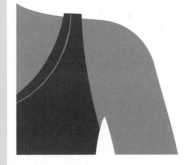

shoulder

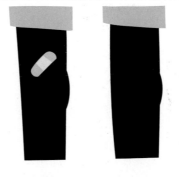

knees

foot

body

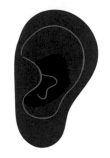

eyes

ears

elbow

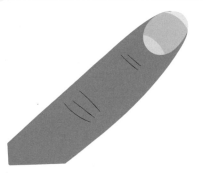

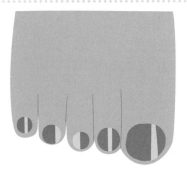

finger

toes

chest

lips

back

face

climbing

skipping

pushing

jumping

hugging

pulling

running

throwing

dancing

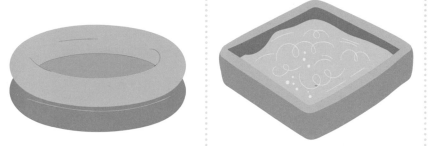

paddling pool

sand pit

roundabout

see-saw

slide

swing

climbing frame

boy

girl

birthday cake

lemonade

ice lolly

pizza

milkshake

biscuit

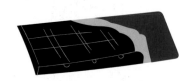

chocolate

sweets

sandwich

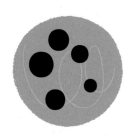

skirt

dress

hat

coat

shirt

pyjamas

shoes

socks

trousers

lion

hippopotamus

bear

elephant

gazelle

giraffe

rhinoceros

crocodile

snake

diver

octopus

dolphin

coral

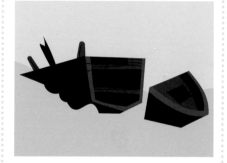

shipwreck

fish

whale

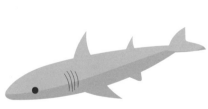

shark

lobster

sea

lighthouse

sand

sun cream

spade

shell

bucket

beach bag

seaweed

beach

rock

beach umbrella

wave

seagull

sky

boat

surfboard

sand castle

crab

37

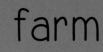

farm

field

apple tree

barn

farmer (man)

farmer (woman)

henhouse

hay

scarecrow

tractor

donkey

horse

cat

sheep

pig

cow

rabbit

goat

chicken

brown hair

red hair

brown eyes

blonde hair

blue eyes

long hair

straight hair

curly hair

short hair

my grandfather

my grandmother

my uncle

my aunt

my mother

my father

my sister

my brother

my cousins

Word list

A actions
aeroplane
alarm clock
alphabet
ambulance
apple
apple tree
apricot
April
arm
armbands
armchair
August
aunt
autumn

B back
bakery
ball
banana
barn
baseball
basketball
bath
bathroom
beach

beach umbrella
beach bag
beanbag
bear
bed
bedroom
beetle
bench
bicycle
big
bin
bird
birthday cake
biscuit
black
blue
boat
body
book
boy
bridge
broccoli
brother
brown
bucket

bus
butcher
butter
C car
car park
carrot
castle
cat
caterpillar
ceiling
celery
chair
cheese
cheesemonger
chest
chest of drawers
chicken
chimney
chocolate
church
cinema
circle
classroom
clean
climb

climbing frame
clock
clothes
cloud
coat
coffee
cold
colouring pencil
colours
comic
computer
coral
costume
courgette
cousins
cow
crab
crocodile
cup of tea
cupboard
curly
curtains
cushion

D dance
December

deer
desk
dirty
diver
diving board
dog
doll
dolphin
donkey
door
dragon
dress
duck

E ears
eggs
eight
eighteen
elbow
elephant
eleven
eyes

F face
fairy
family
farm

farm animals
farmer
fast
father
February
fence
field
fifteen
finger
fire engine
fish
fishmonger
five
floor
flower
fog
foot
football
forest
fork
four
fourteen
fox
fridge
fruit

Word list

G gate
games console
garage
garden
gazelle
giraffe
girl
glue
goat
grandfather
grandmother
grapes
grass
green
green beans
gymnastics
H hair
hand
hat
hay
head
heavy
hedge
hedgehog
henhouse

hexagon
high
hippopotamus
horse
hose pipe
hospital
hot
house
hug
I ice cream
ice lolly
inside
J January
July
June
jump
K kitchen
kite
knees
knife
knight
L ladder
lake
leg
lemonade

lettuce
librarian
library
lifeguard
light
lighthouse
lion
lips
listen
living room
lobster
long
look
low
M March
May
meat
mermaid
messy
milk
milkshake
mirror
money
month
mosque

English

mother
motorbike
mouse
mouth

N nest
nine
nineteen
nose
notebook
November
numbers

O October
octopus
old
on top
once upon a time
one
opposites
orange (colour)
orange (fruit)
outside
oval
oven
owl

P paddling pool

paints
paper
park
party
pasta
path
peach
pear
pen
pencil case
pentagon
picture book
pig
pirate
pizza
playground
police car
post office
poster
potato
princess
pull
purple
push
pyjamas

R rabbit
rain
raspberry
rectangle
red
rhinoceros
rhombus
rice
river
rock
roof
roundabout
rug
rugby
ruler
run

S sand
sand castle
sand pit
sandwich
sausages
scarecrow
scissors
sea
seagull

season
seaweed
see-saw
September
seven
seventeen
shampoo
shapes
shark
sheep
shelf
shell
shipwreck
shirt
shoes
shopping
shopping bag
shopping basket
shopping trolley
short
shoulder
shower
sink
sister
six

sixteen
skateboard
skip
skirt
sky
slide
slow
small
snake
snow
soap
socks
sofa
spade
spoon
sport
spring
square
squirrel
stairs
swim
star
stories
storm
storytime

straight
strawberry
summer
sun
sun cream
supermarket
surfboard
swan
sweetcorn
sweets
swimming
swimming cap
swimming costume
swimming goggles
swimming pool
swing
synagogue
T taxi
teacher
teddy bear
telephone
television
ten
tennis
thirteen

three
throw
tidy
till
toes
toilet
tomato
toothbrush
toothpaste
towel
town
town hall
tractor
train
train station
tree
triangle
trousers
twelve
twenty
two

U uncle
under
unicorn

V vegetables

vehicles

W wardrobe
wave
weather
whale
white
whiteboard
wind
window
winter
witch
worm

Y year
yellow
yoghurt
young

Z zoo

written by Sam Hutchinson

illustrated by Kim Hankinson

Published by b small publishing ltd.

www.bsmall.co.uk

Text & Illustrations copyright © b small publishing ltd. 2018

1 2 3 4 5

ISBN 978-1-911509-74-5

Design: Kim Hankinson   Editorial: Emilie Martin & Rachel Thorpe   Production: Madeleine Ehm

Publisher: Sam Hutchinson

Printed in China by WKT Co. Ltd.